Physical Science in
CYCLING SPORTS

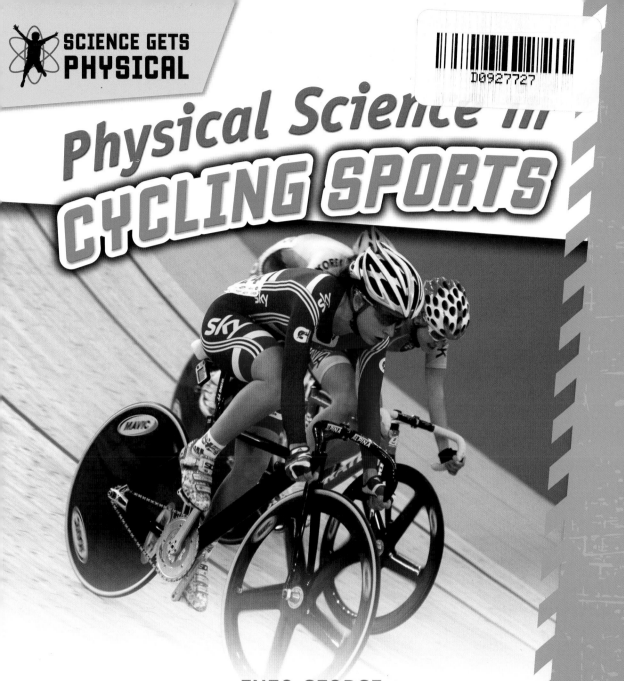

ENZO GEORGE

CRABTREE
PUBLISHING COMPANY
WWW.CRABTREEBOOKS.COM

Author: Enzo George
Editors: Sarah Eason, Jennifer Sanderson,
    and Elizabeth DiEmanuele
Consultant: David Hawksett
Editorial director: Kathy Middleton
Proofreader: Wendy Scavuzzo
Design: Paul Myerscough and Jeni Child
Design edits: Katherine Berti
Cover design: Lorraine Inglis
Photo research: Rachel Blount
Print and production coordinator:
    Katherine Berti

Written, developed, and produced by Calcium

Photo Credits:
t=Top, c=Center, b=Bottom, l= Left, r=Right

Inside: Inside: Flickr: Anders: p. 17; Shutterstock: Africa Studio: p. 27; Ilya Andriyanov: p. 22; Sergei Bachlakov: p. 7, 19; Darren Baker: p. 8; Billion Photos: p. 37; Blue Cat Studio: p. 44; C12: p. 36; Dolomite-summits: p. 6; Elena Elisseeva: p. 45; Florelena: p. 3, 38; Nor Gal: p. 31; Mitch Gunn: p. 1, 35; Sean Heatley: p. 42–43t; HodagMedia: p. 28; Stefan Holm: p. 15; Kuznetcov_Konstantin: p. 5; McKerrell Photography: p. 26; Nithid Memanee: p. 21; Mezzotint: p. 30; Milkovasa: p. 9; Monkey Business Images: p. 4, 24; Ollyy: p. 16; Pavel1964: p. 39; PhilMacDPhoto: p. 42b; Puwanai: p. 34; Rawpixel.com: p. 32; Radu Razvan: p. 12, 23, 40–41; Reimar: p. 11; Oleksiy Rezin: p. 29; Rena Schild: p. 33; Vladyslav Starozhylov: p. 14; Anirut Thailand: p. 20; TorwaiStudio: p. 18, 25; Gaie Uchel: p. 41t; Michael Woodruff: p. 10; Wikimedia Commons: DenP Images: p. 13

Cover: Shutterstock: Eugene Onischenko

Library and Archives Canada Cataloguing in Publication

Title: Physical science in cycling sports / Enzo George.
Names: George, Enzo, author.
Description: Series statement: Science gets physical |
    Includes index.
Identifiers: Canadiana (print) 2019019541X |
    Canadiana (ebook) 20190195428 |
    ISBN 9780778775454 (hardcover) |
    ISBN 9780778776345 (softcover) |
    ISBN 9781427125200 (HTML)
Subjects: LCSH: Cycling—Juvenile literature.
Classification: LCC GV1043.5 .G46 2020 |
    DDC j796.6—dc23

Library of Congress Cataloging-in-Publication Data

CIP available at the Library of Congress

LCCN: 2019043860

Crabtree Publishing Company
www.crabtreebooks.com   1-800-387-7650

Printed in the U.S.A./012020/CG20191115

Published in Canada
Crabtree Publishing
616 Welland Ave.
St. Catharines, Ontario
L2M 5V6

Published in the United States
Crabtree Publishing
PMB 59051
350 Fifth Avenue, 59th Floor
New York, New York 10118

Published in the United Kingdom
Crabtree Publishing
Maritime House
Basin Road North, Hove
BN41 1WR

Published in Australia
Crabtree Publishing
Unit 3 - 5 Currumbin Court
Capalaba
QLD 4157

CONTENTS

CHAPTER 1

SCIENCE ON TWO WHEELS

Bicycles are everywhere. You might cycle to school or around your neighborhood to visit friends. Cycling is a fun way to get around, and an exciting sport to compete in or to watch. A bike might appear to be a pretty simple machine. But, it is like a science laboratory on wheels. Pedaling on a bicycle uses some of the most complex forces in the world of **physics**.

All About Energy

A bicycle is a machine that converts **energy** from the food you eat into **kinetic energy**, or motion. The bike pedals multiply the **force** you put into pedaling. The force gets moved to the bike rear wheel by a chain. **Gears** at the back wheel multiply the force even more. The force turns the large wheel that then pushes the front wheel and the rest of the bicycle forward.

Almost everyone rides a bike for fun or for getting to school or work.

Bicycle tires are usually quite thin and narrow. The size helps reduce **friction** on the road. But, when you put on the brakes, they use friction to stop the bike safely.

Bicycles are designed to be as efficient as possible. They are usually lightweight. They have a hollow frame that helps even the weight over the two wheels. Some bikes are made from materials that are very strong, but still light enough for you to pick up the bike with a single finger. But, there are different kinds of bikes. If you have a mountain bike (MTB) or a bicycle motocross (BMX) bike, it is likely pretty heavy. These machines get a lot of wear and tear, so they are far more rugged than road bikes.

A Physics Mystery

Physics can explain many things about riding a bicycle, such as why it is harder to ride uphill. But, there is one thing no one can entirely explain: how riding a bike is even possible! A bike should really fall over. There are many ideas that partly explain why it does not, but the overall question is still a mystery!

Mountain bikes can do jumps that ordinary bikes cannot do. But, like all bikes, they still have to follow the laws of physics.

A Range of Bikes

What do you think of when you hear the word "cycling"? You might think of riding to school on a bicycle with racks on the back for your books. Or a foldaway commuter bike with small wheels. It might be a bicycle with drop handlebars and thin tires that speeds along the road or around an oval track. All are bicycles. They all have two wheels and are powered by the rider's legs. But they are adapted to their purpose, so they appear quite different.

Roads and Tracks

Road bikes usually have quite big wheels, up to about 2.9 inches (7.4 cm) across. They are designed to ride over smooth roads, are quite light but strong, and usually have gears. These gears have three **sprockets**, or cogs, at the front of the chain and up to 10 sprockets on the rear wheel. Racing bikes have drop handlebars that curl under at the ends, so the rider can crouch down. Bicycles for daily riding often have straight handlebars that allow the rider to have a more comfortable "sitting up" position.

A track bike is often the same shape as a road bicycle. But, it is made for racing around an indoor or outdoor oval track called a velodrome. Track bikes have no gears, so the pedals are attached to a single cog on the back wheel. This helps reduce **mass**, or weight, so that the bikes are as fast as possible. Track bikes also have no brakes. They stop when the rider stops pedaling.

Riders going uphill often stand up. They do this so that they can use their body weight to push down on the pedals.

MTB and BMX

Mountain bikes are usually a little smaller than road bikes, but they have stronger frames to travel over rocky surfaces. Some have springs and other forms of **suspension** built into the frames. Suspension helps to absorb shocks from the uneven ground. The main difference is the wide and heavy tires. These have thick **treads** to gain a grip on slippery ground.

BMX bikes use smaller wheels. These wheels are about 20 inches (51 cm). They have high-rise handlebars and a single gear. They have a frame of lightweight aluminum tubes, and the wheels are farther apart. This helps provide more stability. The top bar is low, so that riders do not injure themselves when landing after a jump.

BMX bikes have small wheels so they can **accelerate** quickly and be strong enough to handle landing after repeated jumps.

GETTING PHYSICAL: THE VELODROME

A velodrome is an arena built for track racing. The track is an 820-foot (250 m) oval with two straights at the sides, and banked, or sloping, turns at each end. The banking allows riders to keep their bikes at a right angle to the floor, while they are going through the turns. This means that they do not have to slow down. They keep pedaling at full speed, without having to steer. The banking is usually about 45 degrees. On shorter tracks, it can be steeper. The straights are also banked at about 10 to 15 degrees. Around the inside of the track, painted lines mark the shortest route around the track. This lets the riders know the best route to take.

Staying Upright

Learning to ride a bicycle is not as easy as it looks. Once you learn, however, a bike seems very stable. Whenever you stop, the bike becomes unbalanced and you need to put a foot down to keep it upright. A bike does not stand up on its own unless it is moving.

A Question of Balance

Balancing a bike seems quite simple, but, in fact, it is a mystery. Scientists think they largely understand why a bicycle stays upright. But, there are things that they still do not understand. For example, a bike's wheels are set in a straight line and are thinner than the rest of the bike, so they do not provide a stable base for a **stationary** bike. There is no perfect point at which the still bike will balance. As soon as the bike wobbles to one side or another, the force of **gravity** pulls it toward the ground, making it fall.

It can take time to learn how to ride a bike. People say that once you have learned, you never forget.

Getting Dynamic

When a rider pedals a bike, other forces help keep the bike upright. The study of the forces affecting moving objects is called dynamics. According to dynamics, the most important change is when the wheels begin to turn. This generates a **gyroscopic effect**. A gyroscope is a wheel that spins rapidly on an **axis**. When you tilt the wheel in one direction, the force of the spin corrects the balance in the other direction.

The same thing happens when a bike begins to lean over. The spinning front wheel steers the handlebars in the direction of the lean. This brings the wheel back under the bike, keeping it upright.

In addition, the front **forks** are designed to angle forward. The forward angle helps with the bike's direction. The wheel touches the ground slightly behind the **steering axis**. The angle and touch to the ground creates a force that drags the wheel into line. The effect is the same as a shopping cart. Both follow the direction they get pushed.

A third element of stability is weight distribution. A bicycle frame evens the weight of the rider. It moves the **center of mass** to the front wheel. This presses down on the wheel and makes it harder for the wheel to turn off course.

When cornering at speed, a rider must be careful not to lean too far, because the wheels may slip and skid on the road surface.

Dynamics are complex enough for a bike traveling in a straight line. They are even more complex once the bike begins to turn. The rider steers the bike by turning the handlebars, which act as **levers** that multiply the force of the rider's arms and move the front wheel.

As soon as the bike starts to turn, it leans over. A lean to the right causes the bike to turn to the right. As this happens, the rider uses the handlebars to keep applying a **torque**, or turning force, to the left. If they do not do this, the bike will not stay in the turn. Instead, it will go straight. It sounds strange but it is true: if you want to go right, you need to steer to the left.

Some bicycle stunts are complicated. They need special bikes that have no gears, so that one turn of the pedals creates one turn of the wheel. This gives the rider more control over tricks. The stunt form of BMX riding includes massive jumps and twists. The laws of physics can help us understand these tricks.

BMX stunts include full somersaults or flips in the air. These tricks can only be achieved with special ramps.

On the Back Wheel...

One of the most common stunts is a wheelie, where the rider pulls the front wheel off of the ground and rides on their back wheel only. This looks challenging, but in physics it is simple. When a bicycle is on two wheels, gravity pulls on its center of mass, while "normal force" works the other way. For example, these forces push up from the ground on the wheels. Normal force is the force that the ground (or any surface) pushes back up with when we touch it. To lift the front wheel off the ground, the rider has to accelerate and pull up on the handlebars. Doing that takes away the weight from the front **axle**. This increases the torque on the rear axle, which causes the bike frame to rotate into the air.

...and the Front Wheel!

Another common stunt is the stoppie. The stoppie is when the rider raises the back wheel high in the air by suddenly using the front brake. The stoppie is caused by the forward energy of the bike. When you use the brake, the front wheel stops moving. But the law of the **conservation** of energy says that the bicycle's energy cannot be created or destroyed. It has to go somewhere else. The back wheel of the bike still has energy, so it "tries" to continue moving forward. Since it is blocked by the bike frame and the rider, it goes up in the air.

For a skilled rider, it is possible to turn the stoppie into an "endo." An endo is when the bike stays balanced on its front wheel. This involves careful control of the rider's center of mass. The bike goes up in the air above the very small balancing point on the front wheel.

This cyclist is performing a stoppie. Some bikes have tubes on the axle of the front wheel to support the rider's feet during tricks such as stoppies.

SCIENCE WINS!

THE EINSTEIN FLIP

In 2005, Helen Czerski of Cambridge University used physics to design a BMX stunt. She called this stunt the Einstein flip. She used computer models to study what would happen if a rider hit ramps at different angles and speeds. She learned how fast a rider would need to do a rolling backward somersault. This is when the rider tucks in the bike while upside-down.

Ben Wallace tried the stunt. Before he did, Czerski calculated that he had to cycle at 20 miles per hour (32 kph) from a 6-foot (1.8 m) ramp to complete the loop. Ben did it and landed safely on the first try!

On Tour

For many cycling fans, the purest form of racing is a classic stage race. In this race, riders compete almost daily for around three weeks in different stages. There are mountain stages that climb three or four steep peaks in a day. There are long, flat stages that end in a sprint. There are short time trials, where individuals or teams race on their own against the clock. At the end of the race, the rider with the shortest time wins.

Spectators crowd the high mountain roads to watch cyclists at the limits of their strength.

Tour de France

Many countries host their own classic bike race. But, the most famous race is the Tour de France. This race has been around since 1903 and only stopped during the two world wars. Riders set out to cycle more than 2,200 miles (3,500 km) over 21 days, with just two rest days. In 2018, 176 riders started the race. Only 145 finished, as a result of crashes, injuries, and tiredness. Races like the Tour are a good example of the basic science behind cycling. A bike is a machine that changes the energy the rider gains from food into kinetic energy. The bike multiplies the rider's effort into forward speed. There are many forces that slow down the bike. When cycling uphill, the force of gravity pulls on the bike. When cycling quickly, **air resistance** pushes against the cyclist's body. As the wheels turn, parts of the tire squish against the road. This is known as **rolling resistance**. Keeping the bike moving requires a lot of energy.

Fueling the Body

Riders in the Tour de France eat and drink a lot! They have to consume about five thousand calories for every stage. At the mountain stage, they consume up to seven thousand calories! There is not enough time to eat and digest so much energy in normal food, because it would be too bulky. Cyclists have to consume special gels and drinks during the stage. They consume about 8.8 ounces (250 g) of carbohydrate for energy every hour, for example. This is close to the body's largest consumption. If a cyclist falls behind by missing a meal or an energy bar, it is almost impossible to catch up again. This leads to a calorie shortage. This means the body is using more energy than it receives from food. If they do not take in enough calories, it can harm their performance.

SCIENCE WINS!

BIG MIG

The Spaniard Miguel Induráin (in the leader's yellow jersey) won the Tour de France five times in the early 1990s. Part of his success was how his body functioned. His lungs could take in about 2.1 gallons (8 l) of air. This meant that his blood could carry 1.8 gallons (7 l) of oxygen around his body every minute. The average is half of that. This oxygen helped muscles. The result was that he improved his ability to climb mountains, a big part of winning a classic stage race.

CHAPTER 2

SHAPE OF THE BIKE

In 2005, the bicycle was voted the best invention in the history of the world. That might seem surprising. But, the bike is efficient at moving the energy it uses into kinetic energy. The bike was the first machine that let humans travel fast on land without the help of another source of power, such as a horse pulling a cart.

Every bike is made of the same basic parts: frame, wheels, saddle, handlebars, and **crankset**.

Simple...but Complicated

The bicycle is simple. There are two wheels, which are usually held together by a frame of hollow tubes. There is a saddle to sit on and handlebars at the front, which turn to steer the wheels. At the bottom of the frame is the crankset: two pedals attached to an axis that turns a large chainring. The chainring transfers energy by a chain to smaller sprockets on the axis of the rear wheel. This turns the rear wheel and pushes the front wheel forward. At the front of the bike, the headset joins the frame to the handlebars.

Sounds simple? Over time, every part of the bike has improved at turning human effort into motion. The tubes of the frame are lightweight and hollow. They are also set at angles to create triangles that give the frame strength and flexibility. The arrangement of the saddle and handlebars make the rider lean forward. The lean helps the rider spread out their weight. The forks that hold the front wheel are also angled to keep the bike stable.

The Wheels

The wheels have metal rims that are attached to the central **hub** by thin spokes. This keeps the wheels light, but also makes them very strong. The spokes help spread the bicycle and rider's weight over the whole wheel and keep it sturdy. The taller the wheel, the more it multiplies the effort put into turning the pedals. Gears on the rear wheel also multiply effort. They reduce the amount of effort needed to cycle uphill. There are brakes on both wheels that work by squeezing pads against the rims to keep the wheels from turning.

The wide handlebars of an MTB push the rider's arms apart. This widens the rider's mass and creates more stability.

Under Stress

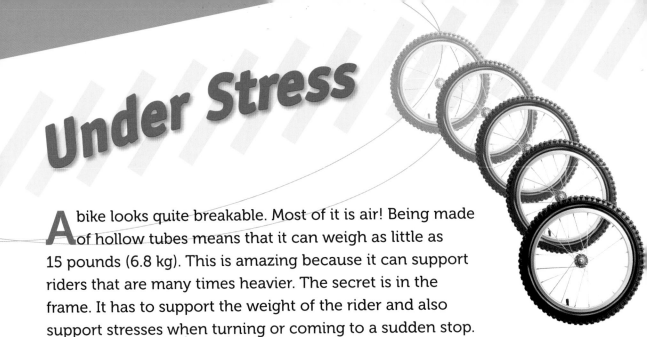

A bike looks quite breakable. Most of it is air! Being made of hollow tubes means that it can weigh as little as 15 pounds (6.8 kg). This is amazing because it can support riders that are many times heavier. The secret is in the frame. It has to support the weight of the rider and also support stresses when turning or coming to a sudden stop.

Triangles for Strength

Think of a bicycle. What shape is the frame? The chances are that it is like a triangle, with a top tube or crossbar. There is also a seat tube that goes from the seat down to the pedals. Finally, a down tube joins the pedals to the front of the top bar.

The reason the frame is this shape is because a triangle is naturally strong. Its sides all push onto one another and **reinforce** each other. This means that it is difficult for one side to collapse under stress. There is a second triangular shape behind the seat tube that supports the rear wheel.

On a steep slope, the bike's frame transfers downward pressure onto the rear wheel.

The two triangles create a diamond, where all the tubes provide strength. The tubes are usually welded together. Welding is when the metal is melted and joined together. The final joins are very strong but also flexible. The frame can take in bumps and twists as the bike travels. If the bike was **rigid**, it might break.

Weight Distribution

The angle of the frame supports the rider's weight. Even though the rider sits at the back, they lean forward. This lean moves their center of gravity forward. The lean also evens out their weight over the two wheels. Balancing the rider's weight is important. For example, going uphill with too much weight on the rear wheel would make the bike tip backward.

SCIENCE WINS!

GRAEME BUILDS A BIKE

In 1993, Scottish cyclist Graeme Obree (shown above) set out to break a world record. He wanted to bike the greatest distance ever cycled in an hour. He was unhappy with the bicycles available to ride, so he designed and built his own. He called this bike Old Faithful. It had no top bar, so Obree would not hit his knees, and also had narrow handlebars that he held beneath his chest. These handlebars kept his elbows tucked in at his sides. Obree used **bearings** from a washing machine. He believed that if a washing machine could spin at 1,200 revolutions per minute (rpm), the bearings must be good. Riding this bike, Obree set a record of 32.060 miles (51.596 km).

Materials

Bicycle designers use the best materials to make frames that are light and strong. Materials cannot be too rigid. A flexible bike frame absorbs the **impact** of a bumpy surface. It also makes bumps easier on the rider. Some bikes have springs built into them. The springs make the bike better at absorbing shock, so it spreads evenly through the frame.

Hollow Tubes

By making the frame hollow, the weight of the bike is reduced, so it is easier to pedal. Although the tubes are hollow, they are strong. They are usually welded to each other. The most common material is lightweight steel. This material is made by combining iron with a small amount of carbon and other metals. Steel is strong and is easily repaired if it is dented or bent. But, it can rust if it is exposed to wetness.

Modern bikes need frequent maintenance.

Other Materials

Aluminum is lighter than steel, but it is not as strong, so aluminum tubes are often fatter than steel tubes. Because aluminum is so soft, it can easily be damaged and is more difficult than steel to repair. Aluminum corrodes slowly because **corrosion** creates a layer of aluminum oxide that protects the aluminum, preventing further corrosion.

Titanium is lighter than steel. Titanium tubes are made fatter to give the frame more strength. Magnesium is also light, but it is highly **reactive**. It needs to be mixed with other metals. It must also be carefully coated with protective chemicals. Otherwise, it is quick to corrode.

One of the most popular modern materials for bike frames is carbon fiber. Carbon fiber is an artificial material based on carbon **atoms**. It is very light and very strong. It is not only used for bikes, but is the same material used to make many airplanes. All parts of a bike can be made from carbon fiber, but the material has to be held together with a glue-like material called epoxy resin. Without epoxy resin, carbon fiber is brittle and would likely crack.

For strength, BMX bike frames are often made from chromoly steel. This is steel that has been strengthened by adding chromium and molybdenum.

CHAPTER 3

ON A ROLL

The wheels give the bike its name. The Latin prefix "bi" means "two," so bicycle means "having two wheels." A tricycle has three wheels, with "tri" meaning "three." Wheels come in different sizes, depending on what the bike is being used for. The biggest wheels are on racing bikes. These wheels increase the effort of the cyclist's legs the most. Smaller wheels, such as on BMX bikes, are more stable and grip better on loose surfaces. Children's bikes may use very small wheels, because they do not need a lot of speed.

Parts of a Wheel

A wheel is made up of a hub, which turns around a fixed axle. The hub contains ball bearings, which sit in grease so they turn smoothly over the axle. The hub is connected by spokes to a thin, circular wheel rim, which holds a rubber tire. The spokes look breakable. But they are made to make the wheel very strong. The tire is inflated with air, which provides a smooth ride without too much friction. The air also absorbs some of the shock from the road surface.

Tricycles are far more stable than bicycles. But, increased friction from the third tire and the non-**aerodynamic** shape make them heavier to pedal.

The rear forks are shaped to fit clusters of gears that might have up to 10 sprockets of different sizes.

The wheels and tires can be very thin on some racing bikes. Thinner wheels reduce the surface of the tire in contact with the road. But, on an MTB, the wheels and tires are much wider, which increases the amount of grip on uneven ground.

Front and Rear

The rear wheel provides the power that moves the bike. It has a cluster of gears linked by a chain to the crankset. As the wheel turns, the outside of the tire grips the ground. The friction allows the bike to push forward. This force pushes along the frame, which in turn makes the front wheel spin. The front wheel is attached to the front forks. Its central hub contains ball bearings. These ball bearings allow the wheel to rotate against the fixed axle. Ball bearings have a large surface area, which distributes the load as the wheel turns.

A spoked bike wheel often supports up to about 400 times its own weight. That makes them incredibly strong. In fact, it makes them among the strongest devices humans have ever invented!

Axles and Spokes

When drawing bicycle wheels, most people draw spokes that come out from the hub in the middle. We often picture bikes this way. But, if spokes were really made like this, the wheel would not work as well. The bike would be hard to pedal.

At a Tangent

To make the rear wheel stronger, the spokes are usually set at an angle. The angle stops the spoke from running at a 90 degree angle from the hub to the rim. The angles allow the wheel to transfer the torque that makes the wheel turn. The spokes pull the wheel inward. This pull gives it rotary motion rather than forward linear, or straight-line, motion. The spokes are pulled tight.

There are usually between 20 and 36 spokes in a wheel. The rear wheel often has more spokes than the front. This is because the rear wheel carries more weight from the rider. The spokes of the rear wheel take more stress from torque, as they transmit energy to the rim.

The spokes are attached to a raised lip on the wheel hub called the flange.

Light but Sturdy

The spokes crisscross from one side of the rim to the opposite side of the hub. This helps make the wheel sturdy. The weight of the rider spreads through the spokes as the wheel turns. But, the weight is not evenly spread. The spokes that are in a vertical position at any time carry most of the load. The spokes in a horizontal position carry the least. The spokes stretch and relax in turn as the wheel spins.

Spokes are designed to be as light as possible and to reduce **drag** from air resistance. Most spokes are round. But, some bikes have oval or flat spokes to try to make it even easier for the spokes to pass through the air. The most common material for spokes is stainless steel, which is strong and resistant to corrosion and rust. It is also cheaper.

The British cyclist Bradley Wiggins used a solid rear wheel and a three-spoked front wheel to reduce drag in a time trial during the Tour de France in 2012. Wiggins won the race that year.

Not all bicycle wheels have spokes. When a rider needs to go at the highest speed, some riders use rear wheels that are solid disks. Solid wheels are heavier than spoked wheels, but they have the advantage of reducing air resistance. Air resistance becomes a bigger problem the faster a bike goes. At high speeds, the spokes are passing through the air so quickly that they create their own **eddies** in the air. These eddies come together to increase air resistance. The amount of resistance is still tiny, but over a race, it could mean the difference between victory or defeat by a tenth of a second.

Freewheeling

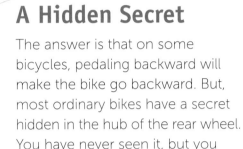

A great trick when learning to ride a bike is to pedal fast, then let the bike roll forward. You can freewheel or even pedal backward. You will still move forward. If you think about it, though, why does pedaling backward not make the bicycle go backward, too?

A Hidden Secret

The answer is that on some bicycles, pedaling backward will make the bike go backward. But, most ordinary bikes have a secret hidden in the hub of the rear wheel. You have never seen it, but you might have heard it.

When you are coasting, there is a ticking sound from the rear wheel. It is the sound of two small struts, called pawls, which are attached to the axle that runs across the teeth of a cogged wheel inside the hub. This is called a ratchet. A ratchet can produce rotation in one direction, but not in the other. When the pedals are turning forward, the pawls catch in the ratchet and turn the wheel. When the pedals are still or turning backward, the pawls separate from the ratchet. The ratchet stays still, while the wheel continues to roll forward.

Freewheeling might look simple. But, it is not possible without engineering!

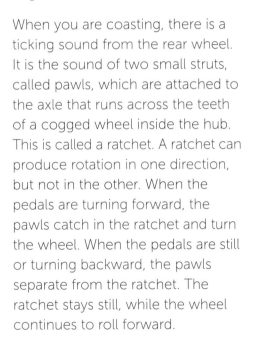

Aerodynamic Positions

Some people try all sorts of positions to go faster when they freewheel downhill. Once a bike is freewheeling, there are only two things that determine its **velocity**, or how fast it goes: the weight of the rider and the amount of air resistance slowing down the bike. By squatting down over the crossbar, some riders try to take up less space. This helps them become more aerodynamic. Others stand up on their pedals and drop their heads to make their backs flatter. Despite these tricks, the weight of the rider does the most for the speed of the bike. Also, some of the tricks are dangerous when you are going fast.

Some riders hunch so much to reduce air resistance that they press their chests down on their handlebars.

GETTING PHYSICAL: ROLLING RESISTANCE

When you are freewheeling, the biggest drag that slows down the bike comes from the ground. This is called rolling resistance. Only a small part of the tire is in contact with the ground at any time. But, that part is affected by friction that slows it down as it turns. Also, the part of the tire on the ground has a lot of the rider's weight. This squeezes some air into other parts of the tube. The tire changes, so that more of it touches the ground. All of this increases rolling resistance. For this reason, no matter how fast you are going, the bike will slow down and eventually come to a stop.

Burning Rubber

Getting a puncture is a problem. You have to fix the inner tube with a kit or even fit a new one. You might wonder if it would be easier to have bikes that do not have blow-up tires. But, a bike without air in the tires would be uncomfortable and hard to pedal.

Extra-wide tires with a chunky grip make it possible to ride over a slippery surface such as snow.

A Load of Air

Cycling only really became popular in the late 1800s when people learned how to use rubber to make tires that are filled with air. A rubber tire usually contains a much thinner circular tube to hold the air. This is called an inner tube. Air is pumped into the tube through a small valve that sticks out through the wheel rim.

The Shape of a Tire

The tire itself has two thinner walls that fit inside flanges on the wheel rim and a thicker tread. The tread is the part that makes contact with the ground. Treads can be designed for speed or for grip. For racing on smooth roads or on a track, the tires often do not have any tread.

Different types of treads are designed for different weather and surfaces.

The high air pressure reduces the give when the tire is pushed against the road. This keeps up a high speed and allows the bike to roll more easily for every turn of the pedals. However, it makes the bike less stable on a bumpy surface. On an MTB, the tires are wider and have a lot of grip. They are also inflated to a lower pressure, so that they squash a little as they touch the ground. The tire spreads out and shapes to the surface. This gives better grip, but makes it more difficult to travel quickly.

The Middle Way

Most regular bicycles have tires that are somewhere in the middle in terms of pressure. These tires have some tread to help them stick to the road in wet conditions or to go off-road on dirt tracks or grass. Tires usually have a recommended pressure stamped on the tire in pounds per square inch (psi). This is the amount of force the air applies to each square inch of the inside of the tube.

GETTING PHYSICAL: TREAD

The quickest tires have no grip. They are called slicks, because they are thin and smooth. In the rain, they can be dangerous. If a film of water forms between the tire and the road, the bicycle can aquaplane. This means it slides as though it were on ice because there is no friction. Many road tires have some patterns of grooves on them. These grooves are designed to squeeze out water from the sides of the tires as they pass over the ground. The tires create more friction, which makes them a bit slower. For MTB and BMX, riders use thicker tires with heavier treads. This helps grip in muddy or stony conditions.

CHAPTER 4

GENERATING POWER

The first bicycles had no pedals. The riders pushed themselves along the ground with their feet. The turning wheels still helped riders travel faster, but they could not travel at high speeds. Fast bicycles did not become available until the invention of the safety bicycle. For the most part, the safety bicycle is what we now call a bicycle. The safety bicycle uses pedals that are attached to the rear wheel by a chain. There are also gears or sprockets.

Get in Gear

In the early days of cycling, the only way to make a bike go faster was to have bigger wheels. That led to the development of the penny farthing, which had a huge front wheel up to 5 feet (1.5 m) in diameter and a tiny back wheel. That changed with the invention of chains and gears. Gears multiply the force generated as the rider pedals, and transmit that force to the rear wheel. As that wheel turns, it pushes the bike and the front wheel.

Penny farthings were named after two coins of the day: the larger penny and the smaller farthing, worth a quarter of a penny.

28

The Crankset

A bike converts reciprocal motion into rotational motion. Reciprocal motion is the up-and-down motion of the rider's legs. Rotational motion is turning motion. This conversion takes place in the crankset, which is at the front end of the chain.

The crankset includes the two pedals and the arms, or cranks, which join them to their hub. The crankset has one or more sprockets or chainrings. These rings have teeth spaced around the outside. They fit into the links of a continuous chain as it passes over them. The chain is made of small hollow links that are hinged to let the links bend as they pass around the chainring. The teeth pull the chain. As this happens, the teeth keep the chain tense and pull on a small sprocket (attached to the hub of the rear wheel). This causes the rear wheel to turn.

The Drivetrain

Bicycle drivetrain is the name for the whole system that moves the rider's power to forward motion. Most bicycles use the same design, but there are a few kinds of drivetrains. For example, some bikes are powered by the arms rather than the legs. Tandems also allow two riders to power the drivetrain at the same time, generating more power and higher speeds. In recumbent bikes, riders sit or lie down with their legs in front of them. These bicycles may look very different from the usual bikes, but their drivetrains work in the same way.

Gearing Up

You are out for a bike ride when you find yourself rolling along a brand-new piece of road. It is flat and empty, and the road is smooth. You click the gear levers to get you into the highest gear you have. The highest gear is the biggest cog at the front and the smallest cog at the back. You start pushing with your legs and feel the tires begin to hum. This is the thrill of propelling yourself along as fast as you can.

Cogs and Ratios

Gears turn the effort you put into pedaling into the greatest amount of work for the bike wheels. Without gears, turning the pedals once would turn the back wheel once. The truth is that the outside wheel travels farther than the pedals do with one spin. This happens because of their different sizes. If you add different sized gears, it is possible to increase the power more. The difference between the number of cogs on the front and back is called the gear ratio.

Some riders give up on pedals and gears. Instead, they use electric bikes with small motors to ride up hills.

Understanding the gear ratio is simple. For example, think of a bike that has three rings at the front and seven at the back. This bike would have 21 different gear ratios available (3 x 7 = 21). For a gear ratio of 5:1, the back wheel will turn five times when the pedals turn once. On a normal-sized bike, that is a distance of about 35 feet (10.7 m) from a single turn of the pedal.

Turn, Turn, Turn

Such a gear ratio is very difficult to pedal if you are not already going fast, and is impossible to use uphill. That is why there are ratios that are close to 1:1. In these ratios, the back wheel will move just once with every turn of the pedals, which makes it easier to pedal as fast as possible. The speed at which the pedals turn is called the **cadence**. A higher cadence keeps **momentum** in the legs and bike. It may sound a little strange, but it is easier to pedal faster with less effort than a bit slower with more effort.

GETTING PHYSICAL: CHAIN GANG

The cluster of gear sprockets on the back wheel of a bike is known as a cassette. The device that moves the chain from one cog to another is called the derailleur.

The derailleur on the rear wheel operates on the bottom part of the chain. The top part is under tension from moving power from the pedals to the wheel. The derailleur keeps the bottom of the chain under lighter tension. This tension lets it move from side to side as the derailleur arm moves. The two pulleys on the derailleur arm drag the chain left or right, where it catches on the next sprocket in the cassette.

A cassette can have 10 or more sprockets.

Pedals and Levers

A bicycle is really a series of levers. Levers are long rods that pivot around a fulcrum, or turning point, to increase a force. For example, bicycle handlebars are levers. They are long and they magnify the effort of the rider. With handlebars, it does not take much effort to move the front wheel to steer. On an MTB, the arms work as levers to pull the front wheel off the ground to climb over obstacles.

Doing the Legwork

The most important levers on a bike are the pedals and cranks. The pedals are set at 180 degrees to each other, so that one points up while the other points down. They have hinges so they remain flat at all times as they turn the cranks up and down. The cranks convert the up-and-down force of the cyclist's legs into rotary motion. Professional cyclists attach their feet to the pedals by wearing shoes with **cleats**. These shoes anchor into slots on the pedals. The result is a more stable ride. The profile of the rider becomes like a triangle with a point at the top and a wider base.

Clipping their feet to the pedals with cleats means a cyclist can apply power when pushing down and pulling up on the pedal.

Generating Power

The efficiency of a cyclist is measured by how much power they create through the pedals. Power depends on the force and speed that turn the pedals. This gets measured in units called watts. If a cyclist wants to go faster, they can either push harder on the pedals or increase the speed they pedal.

A racing position allows the rider to generate maximum power by using their thigh muscles, which are some of the largest muscles in the body.

GETTING PHYSICAL: CADENCE

Good cyclists like to keep up a high cadence. As you have read, cadence is the number of times the pedals get turned in a minute. For a regular rider, this is about 60 to 80 rpm, or rotations per minute. For professional cyclists, it rises to between 80 and 120 rpm. This allows riders to keep the same forward velocity without having to use all of their effort.

CHAPTER 5

PUT ON THE BRAKES

Sooner or later, cyclists need to stop. That means they need good brakes, not just to come to a graceful halt but also to avoid accidents. Most people who have ridden a bike have fallen off once or twice. Brakes help make sure that does not happen too often!

Rim Brakes

Brakes usually take the form of **calipers**. Calipers are two arms joined by a hinge or by the brake cable running from the handlebars. Each arm carries a block of rubber. When the cyclist squeezes the brakes, the calipers push against the rim of the wheel, below the tire. This creates friction, which slows down the wheel until it stops. This part of the wheel is traveling much quicker than the part near the hub, but it has less force. That makes it easy for the brakes to stop the wheel.

Side-pull cantilever brakes, or V-brakes, are pulled together by a single cable that joins the two arms at the top.

Disk Brakes

Disk brakes work closer to the hub. When you pull the brake lever, the cable pulls a caliper attached to one of the front forks. This caliper pushes a brake pad against a disk called the rotor.

The rotor is attached to the wheel. This again slows the wheel by friction. It has to work harder than rim brakes, because the hub turns with more force. Some riders prefer disk brakes.

Others find disk brakes heavy and challenging. For example, disk brakes make it harder to change a wheel.

One great advantage of disk brakes over rim brakes is that they work better in wet conditions. If the wheels and rubber brakes are wet or muddy, it can reduce friction between the brake and the wheel rim. This means that the rider has to squeeze the brakes harder, and keep them on longer, to slow the bicycle down.

No Brakes!

Some bicycles have no brakes. These are mainly bikes that have a single gear in which the chain is attached directly to the rear hub. For example, track bikes have no brakes to keep them as light as possible. Some stunt bikes also have no brakes. On these bikes, the wheels stop when the rider stops pedaling.

On the track, cyclists can slow down only by turning the pedals more slowly until they stop.

Force of Friction

It is best to apply the brakes smoothly. You can use the front and back brakes at the same time. If you apply the back brake too hard, the wheel will lock, but the bike's forward movement will continue. The law of the conservation of energy says that you cannot destroy the forward energy of the bike. The forward energy must change into other forms of energy. In this case, the forward energy will cause the back wheel to skid or drag over the surface of the ground, until friction brings the bike to a stop. The energy goes to generate heat through friction, as well as wear away the tire.

If you hit the front brake too hard, the result is worse. The bike's kinetic energy is blocked from creating forward motion, so the energy travels upward. This creates torque that sends the back wheel up into the air, throwing the rider over the handlebars.

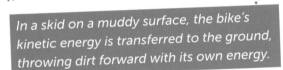

In a skid on a muddy surface, the bike's kinetic energy is transferred to the ground, throwing dirt forward with its own energy.

Creating Heat

When the brakes are applied smoothly, most of the energy changes into heat. If you ever feel your brake pads just after you have come to a stop, they will be warm. The friction of rubbing on the wheel rim creates heat on the pads, which then passes into the air. Rubber is a good **insulator**, so it does not pass the heat to the rest of the bike.

Under extreme pressure, disk brakes on MTBs can get very hot. Sometimes on downhill runs, riders can smell burning at the bottom. Some people say they have seen the rotor wheel glowing red when it has become too hot through rubbing against the metal brake pad.

A Question of Friction

Friction is the force that happens when two objects rub against each other. The force resists movement. A moving bike is constantly under rolling resistance. This force is just like the friction that tries to slow the motion of the wheels over the ground. The most useful type of friction on a bike happens with braking. This is known as **static friction**. In this case, only the wheel rim moves while the brake blocks do not.

GETTING PHYSICAL: LOSING BALANCE

In a slow bicycle race, the winner is the last person to complete the course. The riders have to stay in their lanes, and are not allowed to touch the ground with their feet.

Riding slowly is very hard. A bike that slows down loses the stability from the gyroscopic force of the turning wheels. Without that stability, the bike and rider become like a thin edge carrying a wide weight. The balancing point is so small that it is nearly impossible to find. So, the bike wobbles from one side to the other until the rider has to put a foot down or fall off.

It is almost impossible to ride a bike very slowly, and it usually results in the rider falling off!

CHAPTER 6

AERODYNAMICS

One of cyclists' greatest enemies is the wind. Cycling straight into a wind takes a lot of effort to get nowhere. Even on an ordinary day, the air plays a huge role in bike riding. The reason is that bikes (especially bike riders) are not very aerodynamic. That means they do not pass smoothly through the **molecules** in the air. Instead, they form a huge obstacle to the air, which presses against them and slows them down.

Professional cyclists form a long line as they try to hide behind the rider in front to reduce air resistance.

Cyclists grip the handlebars on their bikes to tuck their arms into their bodies.

Fighting the Air

The problem becomes worse at high speeds. At speeds of more than 25 miles per hour (40 kph), about 90 percent of a rider's effort goes into overcoming air resistance. That is why racers often ride close to one another. They try to get protection from air resistance using a technique called drafting (see page 42).

Double Handlebars

Most race bikes now have two sets of handlebars built into one. There are wider drop handlebars, which often end in downward-pointing curves. Riders use these for steering. The wider the rider's hands are apart, the more leverage the handlebars create on the front wheel. The drop handlebars pull the cyclist forward over the front part of the bike. This lean gives them a lower profile. The air moves over the rider's bent back. There are also two bars close together that stick straight out in front of the main handlebar.

On long straights, when a cyclist does not have to steer, they can lean forward on these. The lean keeps an aerodynamic body shape but also brings the arms in much closer to the body. This tighter position is far more **streamlined** for races such as time trials in which every second counts.

Keep Warm!

Cyclists riding down the side of a mountain can reach speeds of more than 80 miles per hour (129 kph). When cyclists are going that fast, the mountain air rushing past them can be very cold. The air can feel even colder if they are hot and sweaty from cycling up the mountain. It can even cause their body temperature to fall dangerously low. Many racers grab newspapers from spectators to shove down the fronts of their jerseys. The paper forms a shield. It protects their chests from the wind.

Cutting Drag

Cyclists often wear tight shirts and shorts. These clothes are usually made from a fabric called Lycra, which is a form of spandex.

Smooth Passage

The reason cyclists wear such tight shirts and shorts is to reduce drag. The tight clothes allow air to pass over the body. Spandex combines a textile called polyester with a type of plastic called polyurethane, which makes it stretchy enough to hug the body. It also gives it a very smooth surface that the air slides over. On the track, cyclists wear spandex shirts with long sleeves. The long sleeves help reduce the drag caused by their arms. Most cyclists shave their legs. This is so the air cannot get caught in the hairs.

Cycle clothing hugs the rider's body so that air can pass over it as smoothly as possible.

At high speeds, the way the body passes through the air causes what scientists term a "drag crisis." As the front of the cyclist's arms and legs force the air out of the way, they create areas behind the limbs. These areas have lower air pressure. That reduces aerodynamic drag. As a result, the cyclist travels faster.

Perfect Clothing

Scientists have figured out the best clothes for cyclists to wear. The clothes should be tight and made from a smooth material. They should fit so well that they do not have any wrinkles, which increase drag. Even the seams where clothing is sewed together should be flat. It should run in the direction of travel. The more bare skin that is covered, the less drag.

Tests at the Olympic Games show that the right clothes can improve performance by more than 1.5 percent. This could be the difference between the Olympic silver medal and the gold!

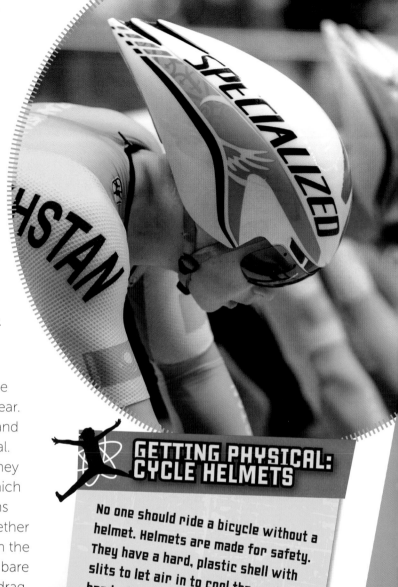

GETTING PHYSICAL: CYCLE HELMETS

No one should ride a bicycle without a helmet. Helmets are made for safety. They have a hard, plastic shell with slits to let air in to cool the cyclist's head. They also have foam pads inside that fit closely to the rider's skull. The plastic shell is designed to shatter on impact. This spreads the shock away from the head. Some cycle helmets are designed as much for speed as for safety. The head is not very aerodynamic. Adding a long tail to the helmet helps prevent the creation of eddies that create drag on the rider.

Drafting

When a small group of cyclists race down the road, most often they line up, one behind the other. They ride close to the cyclist in front. Every now and then, the rider at the front pulls out of the way and drops to the back. They let the next rider take a turn at the front. It is not that they do not want to win. It is because being at the front of the race takes far more energy than following behind. The reason for this is simple: air resistance.

Get in Line

The first cyclist faces the full force of air resistance. But, once he has punched a "hole" in the air, this creates an eddy of lower air pressure behind them. The low air pressure pulls the following cyclist forward, to fill the space. So, the cyclist does not have to cycle so hard. The shorter the distance between riders, the greater the benefit.

Drafting is so efficient that a rider in the center of the group can use up to 40 percent less energy than the leader. When a mass of cyclists ride together, it is called a peloton. In a peloton, it is possible to see riders at the front pedaling hard while those near the back freewheel. That is why cyclists usually take turns riding at the front of the race. It is too tiring to stay there all the time.

Across the Road

When cyclists ride in teams, they try different positions on the road to fight the wind. When they are riding in crosswinds, they form a diagonal line across the road. This is called an echelon. The echelon leaves the lead riders fighting the wind. The rest of the team is sheltered. That allows riders to save their energy for their time at the front of the pack.

The Sky cycling team ride together in the Tour de France.

The riders of one team, in green, do all the hard work. They lead the peloton in a road race.

SCIENCE WINS!

SPRINT TO THE END!

One of the most exciting spectacles in cycling is a sprint finish. The best sprinters fight it out with only 656 feet (200 m) to go. But, the preparation starts more than 6 miles (10 km) earlier. The sprinter's team gathers near the front of the race. They use drafting to protect the sprinter and a few others from the wind. Only four bikes back, the rider needs to use just 64 percent of the energy of the front rider.

The teammates take turns riding at the front, keeping up the speed to leave other teams behind. By 1.2 miles (2 km) from the finish, they are tired. They move to one side, leaving their fresher teammates to take turns riding at the front. The goal is to keep the sprinter as fresh as possible. Each rider drops back once their job is done. By the last straight, there is usually one cyclist left. They "pull" the sprinter with them at full speed, until the sprinter times a surge to break off and cross the line.

GET PHYSICAL!

In this experiment, you will learn about what happens to a bike's wheels when you steer around a corner. The experiment is easier with at least two people. Find a friend or a group of friends to help you.

YOU WILL NEED:

- Bicycle
- Large, flat area with a smooth stone surface
- Puddle, or a bucket of water
- Roll of paper towels, if possible
- Video camera or phone camera for filming

Instructions

1. If you are using paper towels, lay a strip about 15 feet (4.6 m) long on the ground.

2. Get the wheels of the bike wet. You can do this by riding through the puddle or by splashing water on the ground and riding through it.

3. While the tires are still wet, ride along the strip of paper or over the smooth ground. Make a sharp turn to the left or right. Then straighten up again. Try turning the other way.

4. Study and film the trail the wet tires leave on the paper or stone.

This experiment is fun—you get to ride your bike straight through a puddle!

44

Analysis

What are the differences between the trail of the front wheel and trail of the rear wheel? What happens to the front wheel when you turn?

Conclusion

You may find that before your front wheel turns, it turns slightly in the other direction. This is because riders often move their handlebars a little bit to the left. They do this just before they turn to the right. Turning your handlebars one way moves your weight in the other direction. The bicycle travels with your body. To stay up, you have to steer in the same direction. This is the opposite direction from the original steering motion. The name for this is counter-steering. It explains that riding a bike involves a constant series of moves to keep the bike in a straight line. This is because the bike is always in a state of imbalance.

When you do the experiment, remember to wear a helmet. Never cycle without one!

GLOSSARY

accelerate To speed up

aerodynamic Shaped to reduce drag from the air

air resistance A force that acts in the opposite direction of an object traveling through the air, slowing it down

atoms The smallest particles of matter

axis An imaginary line around which an object rotates

axle A rod that passes through the wheel center

bearings Small metal balls that support turning parts of a machine

cadence The number of times a cyclist turns the pedals in a set time

calipers Two arms that can press together

center of mass The point in the middle of an object's mass

cleats Bolts on the bottom of a cycling shoe

conservation Staying constant

corrosion Wearing away

crankset The parts of a bicycle that change pedaling motion into turning motion

drag A force that opposes an object's motion

eddies Small waves left by objects as they pass through the air

energy The capacity for doing work

force An interaction that changes the motion of something

forks Two blades that hold a bicycle's front wheel

friction The resistance of one object moving over another

gears Toothed wheels that increase or reduce the energy transferred to something

gravity A force that attracts things toward the center of Earth, or toward any other physical body

gyroscopic effect The ability of a spinning wheel to keep a steady direction; the faster a wheel spins, the more stable it is

hub The center of a wheel

impact The action of one object hitting another

insulator A substance that does not allow heat to pass through easily

kinetic energy The energy an object has because of its motion

levers Bars that rest on a fulcrum, used to move loads

mass The quantity of matter in an object (its "weight")

molecules Particles formed by atoms bonding

momentum The quantity of motion of a moving body, measured as a product of its mass and velocity

physics The branch of science that studies materials and energy

reactive Reacting easily with other chemicals

reinforce Strengthen

rigid Stiff and unmoving

rolling resistance The force that resists the rolling of a ball or wheel

sprockets Toothed wheels

static friction The force that keeps objects at rest

stationary Not moving

steering axis The part of a wheel touching the ground that determines the direction of the whole wheel

streamlined Shaped to pass smoothly through air

suspension A system for absorbing shocks in a vehicle

torque The force that causes objects to rotate

treads Raised patterns on tires that help with grip

velocity Speed in a specific direction

46

LEARNING MORE

Find out more about the physics of cycle sports.

Books

Carleton, Kate. *What Happens to Your Body When You Cycle*
  (The How and Why of Exercise). Rosen Central, 2009.

Peppas, Lynn. *Bicycles: Pedal Power* (Vehicles on the Move).
  Crabtree Publishing, 2011.

Perritano, John. *MX Bikes* (MXplosion). Crabtree Publishing, 2008.

Slade, Suzanne. *The Science of Bicycle Racing* (The Science of Speed).
  Capstone Press, 2014.

Websites

Find out how the different elements of the bicycle work at:
www.explainthatstuff.com/bicycles.html

For a series of articles all about cycling, log on at:
www.exploratorium.edu/cycling/index.html

Read about cycling safety at:
www.safekids.org/bike

INDEX